Contents

W0035935

About This Kit

This kit contains the tools and materials you will need to make 4 candy canes: yarn in white, bright red, and wine red; two pipe cleaners; a G/6 (4mm) crochet hook; and a needle.

How to Read the Instructions

Every line starts with the round/row number in bold, and ends with the stitch count in parentheses.

Instructions in square brackets must be repeated the specified number of times before continuing with the remaining instructions of the round or row (if any).

crochet your own
candy cane ornaments

Kati Gálusz

becker&mayer! books

Brimming with creative inspiration, how-to projects, and useful information to enrich your everyday life, Quarto Knows is a favorite destination for those pursuing their interests and passions. Visit our site and dig deeper with our books into your area of interest: Quarto Creates, Quarto Cooks, Quarto Homes, Quarto Lives, Quarto Drives, Quarto Explores, Quarto Gifts, or Quarto Kids.

Published in 2021 by becker&mayer! books, an imprint of The Quarto Group, 11120 NE 33rd Place, Suite 201, Bellevue, WA 98004 USA. **www.QuartoKnows.com**

This book is part of the *Crochet in a Day: Crochet Your Own Candy Cane Ornaments* kit and is not to be sold separately.

becker&mayer! books titles are also available at discount for retail, wholesale, promotional, and bulk purchase. For details, contact the Special Sales Manager by email at specialsales@quarto.com or by mail at The Quarto Group, Attn: Special Sales Manager, 100 Cummings Center Suite 265D, Beverly, MA 01915 USA.

21 22 23 24 25   5 4 3 2 1

ISBN: 978-0-7603-6948-7

Library of Congress Cataloging-in-Publication Data available upon request.

Author: Katalin Gálusz
Photography: Chris Burrows

Printed, manufactured, and assembled in Shenzhen, China, 05/21.

Distributed by:
Quarto UK, The Old Brewery
6 Blundell Street, London N7 9BH, UK
Allen & Unwin
30 Centre Rd, Scoresby VIC 3179, AUS

Image credits: All stock photographs and design elements © Shutterstock

#340100

Abbreviation Chart

CH	CHAIN OR CHAINS
HDC	HALF DOUBLE CROCHET (US) HALF TREBLE CROCHET (UK)
RND	ROUND
SC	SINGLE CROCHET (US) DOUBLE CROCHET (UK)
ST	STITCH OR STITCHES
YO	YARN OVER

Notes on Tools and Materials

YARN

The pattern in this book was designed with worsted weight yarn, but if you want to make more candy canes, you could use any yarn thickness: as long as you choose a matching hook, your project will turn out just as fine, only smaller or bigger than the original. If working with finer yarn, you might have to replace the pipe cleaner with plain wire to fit inside; thicker yarn might require 2-3 strands of pipe cleaners twisted together to hold the cane shape.

HOOK SIZE AND GAUGE

Exact gauge is not important in this project, as long as you work tight enough to create a fabric that's fairly stiff and doesn't gape visibly. To achieve this, you will need a hook size smaller than recommended on the yarn's label. The samples were crocheted with G/6 (4mm) hook, but this is only a guideline; feel free to experiment to find what best suits your crocheting style.

PIPE CLEANERS

Pipe cleaners, sometimes called chenille stems, have a wire core surrounded by soft pile. They are perfect to shape crochet projects because the piles make them less likely to slip out between the stitches than plain wire, and they are also fairly soft and pliable, so not likely to cause any injury. Still, projects containing any kind of wire should be kept out of reach from very young children.

Crochet Stitches and Techniques

This chapter contains a short primer on the techniques you will need to create the candy canes, but if you are new to crochet, I suggest to practice the basics before starting the actual project. Many yarn shops offer classes, or you can look up video tutorials online.

SLIPKNOT

Use this to begin a chain. Make a loop on your yarn a few inches from the end. *(Fig. A)* Insert your hook through the loop and grab the yarn end connected to the skein. Pull the strand through the loop, then tighten the knot. *(Fig. B)*

YARN OVER (YO)

Wrap the yarn around your hook from back to front.

CHAIN (CH)

Make a slipknot first, unless you are in the middle of a piece and already have a loop on your hook. YO, and pull yarn through the loop on hook. Repeat as many times as required. *(Fig. C)*

The loop on the hook doesn't count as chain, so omit it if you are checking the stitch count.

WORKING INTO STITCHES

Every stitch has two strands in a small V shape on top. Insert your hook under both sides of the V unless otherwise specified.

FRONT AND BACK LOOPS

When you look at the V on top of the stitch, the strand closest to you is called the front loop and the strand farthest from you is called the back loop. If you need to work in front loop only, insert your hook under the closest loop only. If you need to work in back loop only, insert your hook under the farthest loop only. *(Fig. D)*

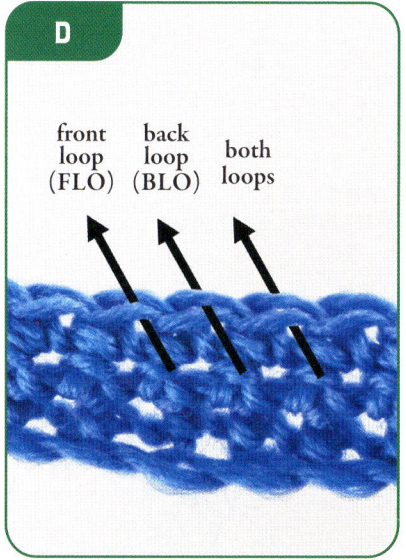

front loop (FLO) back loop (BLO) both loops

SINGLE CROCHET (SC)

Insert your hook into the st or ch, YO and draw up a loop (pull yarn through st or ch). You will have 2 loops on your hook. YO and pull yarn through both loops on hook. *(Fig. E)*

HALF DOUBLE CROCHET (HDC)

YO. Insert your hook into the st or ch, YO and draw up a loop (you will have 3 loops on your hook). YO and pull yarn through all three loops on hook. *(Fig. F)*

SLIP STITCH (SL ST)

Insert your hook into the st or ch, YO and pull yarn through both the st or ch and the loop on hook. Be careful to keep the stitch loose: the V on top should be the same size as the top of other stitches.

E

FASTEN OFF

To finish your piece, cut the yarn 3-4 inches from your hook (or more, if you will need the yarn end for sewing), and pull the end through the last loop on the hook.

CLOSE THE REMAINING HOLE

After fastening off, insert your hook through the front loop of the next st and pull through the yarn end *(Fig. G)*. Repeat in each st around the hole, then pull the end to close the gap. Thread the remaining end in a needle and push through the center, and the seam will become almost invisible. *(Fig. H)*

G

H

WEAVE IN YARN ENDS

In amigurumi, many yarn ends are luckily on the inside of the piece, so we don't have to deal with them. But there is the end left after closing up a body part, as well as the leftover yarn after sewing together pieces. To secure these, stitch through the body several times to catch it in the stuffing. Then pull the yarn tight and cut it right in front of the crochet fabric – the tension will pull it back inside the body.

WORKING IN CONTINUOUS ROUNDS

Amigurumi is mostly crocheted in rounds, starting with a small circle of stitches and progressing in a continuous spiral without turning or joining.

MAGIC RING

The magic ring is a nice technique to start working in the round, because it will create a small circle of stitches with no gap in the center.

Make a circle of the yarn. Insert your hook through this ring *(Fig. I)*, YO and draw up a loop *(Fig. J)*, then ch 1. Work the first round of stitches over both the ring and the free yarn end, then pull on the free end to close the ring.

RIGHT & WRONG SIDE

(Fig. K)(Fig. L) If you are working in rounds without turning, there will be a right and a wrong side. The right side is the side facing you while you work; this should be the outside of your piece. On the right side, individual stitches resemble small Vs. On the wrong side, they are like an upside down V with a horizontal bar on top.

It is quite usual for your work to start curling up in the wrong direction. Stop after the first two or three rounds to check, and if necessary turn the piece right side out.

I

Materials

- 35 YRDS (30M) WHITE WORSTED WEIGHT YARN
- 17 YRDS (15M) LIGHT RED WORSTED WEIGHT YARN
- 17 YRDS (15M) DARK RED WORSTED WEIGHT YARN
- 2 12" (30CM) WHITE PIPE CLEANERS
- G/6 (4MM) CROCHET HOOK

Finished size: 4" (11CM)

Instructions

You will work with two colors simultaneously, switching back and forth between white and red. But there is no need to make any actual color changes, cutting or stranding the unused color – once you get the hang of it it will go almost as fast as working with a single color!

PREPARE THE PIPE CLEANERS

Cut the pipe cleaners in half with a wire cutter if you have one. If you don't, try strong scissors or just keep bending the cleaner at the halfway point, until it breaks apart.

Fold back about 1/4" from each ends of the pieces, so the sharp wire ends will be hidden. *(Fig. A)*

RND 1: With white yarn, make a magic ring and sc 6, pull ring tight

Loosen the live loop on your hook *(Fig. B)*, until it is large enough to tie together with the working yarn *(Fig. C)* - this will prevent the white stitches from unraveling. Do not cut the yarn!

RND 2: Switch to red yarn. Insert your hook into the 1st st of Rnd 1, YO and pull up a loop *(Fig. D)*, then ch 1. Work a sc into the same st *(Fig. E)*, then hdc into the next 5 st. *(Fig. F; Fig. G)*

Loosen the red live loop on your hook, until it is large enough to tie together with the working yarn *(Fig. H)* - this will prevent the red stitches from unraveling. Do not cut the yarn!

Undo the white knot, insert your hook back into the white live loop and tighten it, so you can continue to crochet with white. *(Fig. I)*

RND 3 AND EACH ODD ROUNDS: With white yarn, hdc 6. *(Fig. J; Fig. K)* Then loosen the white live loop, tie it together with the working yarn, undo the red knot and insert your hook into the red live loop. *(Fig. L)*

RND 4 AND EACH EVEN ROUNDS: With red yarn, hdc 6. *(Fig. M)* Then loosen the red live loop, tie it together with the working yarn, undo the white knot and insert your hook into the white live loop.

Continue in this manner until the piece measures about 5 1/2", finishing with an odd (white) round.

LAST EVEN ROUND: With red yarn, hdc 4, sc, sl st. *(Fig. N)* Fasten off the red yarn, then thread the end into a needle and hide it inside the candy cane. *(Fig. O)*

M

LAST ODD ROUND: Undo the knot and insert your hook into the live white loop. *(Fig. P)* Sc 6 *(Fig. Q)*, then fasten off.

Slide a piece of pipe cleaner inside the crochet tube, then use the white yarn end to close the opening. *(Fig. R)*

Bend one end of the tube to create the cane shape. *(Fig. S)*

CANE WITH NARROW RED STRIPES

The pattern is almost identical to the first one, except using sc instead of hdc for the red stripes.

RND 1: With white yarn, make a magic ring and sc 6, pull ring tight

Loosen the live loop on your hook, until it is large enough to tie together with the working yarn - this will prevent the white stitches from unraveling. Do not cut the yarn!

RND 2: Switch to red yarn. Insert your hook into the 1st st of Rnd 1, YO and pull up a loop, then ch 1. Work a sc into the same st, then sc into the next 5 st. *(Fig. T)*

Loosen the red live loop on your hook, until it is large enough to tie together with the working yarn - this will prevent the red stitches from unraveling. Do not cut the yarn!

Undo the white knot, insert your hook back into the white live loop and tighten it, so you can continue to crochet with white.

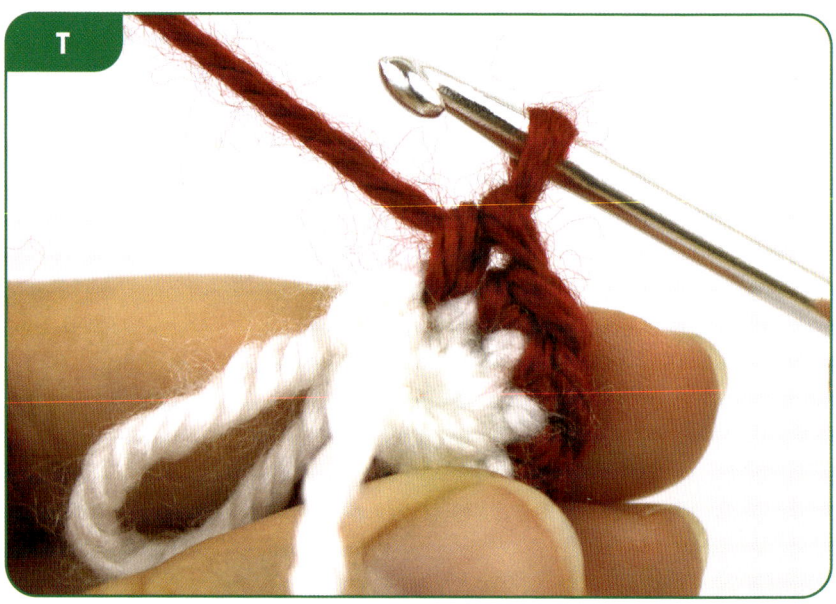

RND 3 AND EACH ODD ROUNDS: With white yarn, hdc 6. Then loosen the white live loop, tie it together with the working yarn, undo the red knot and insert your hook into the red live loop.

RND 4 AND EACH EVEN ROUNDS: With red yarn, sc 6. Then loosen the red live loop, tie it together with the working yarn, undo the white knot and insert your hook into the white live loop. *(Fig. U)*

Continue in this manner until the piece measures about 5 1/2", finishing with an odd (white) round.

LAST EVEN ROUND: With red yarn, sc 5, sl st. *(Fig. V)* Fasten off the red yarn, then thread the end into a needle and hide it inside the candy cane.

LAST ODD ROUND: Undo the knot and insert your hook into the live white loop. Sc 6, then fasten off.

Slide a piece of pipe cleaner inside the crochet tube, then use the white yarn end to close the opening.

Bend one end of the tube to create the cane shape.

Great job! Enjoy your Candy Cane Ornaments!

#CrochetInADay

About the Author

KATI GÁLUSZ discovered the world of amigurumi when she wanted to make a unique gift for a toy-collector friend. What started as a quick fling has grown into the love of a lifetime, allowing her to combine her need for creativity with her two main interests, animals and great books and movies. After lavishing her creations on her long-suffering family and friends, she started to sell them on Etsy and share her crochet patterns on Ravelry. When she is not crocheting, she can be usually found with a book in her hand, surrounded by her dogs in her home near Budapest, Hungary.

ALSO
AVAILABLE

crochet your own
reindeer ornaments

INCLUDES:
- 32-Page Instruction Book
- 5 Colors of Yarn
- Crochet Hook
- Yarn Needle
- Fiberfill
- Safety Eyes

crochet your own
merry and bright baubles

INCLUDES:
- 32-Page Instruction Book
- 6 Skeins of Yarn
- Crochet Hook
- Fiberfill

crochet your own
holly jolly garland

INCLUDES:
- 32-Page Instruction Book
- 3 Colors of Yarn
- Crochet Hook
- Yarn Needle

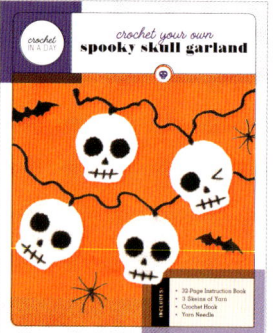

crochet your own
spooky skull garland

INCLUDES:
- 32-Page Instruction Book
- 3 Skeins of Yarn
- Crochet Hook
- Yarn Needle

crochet your own
festive pumpkin

INCLUDES:
- 32-Page Instruction Book
- 3 Colors of Yarn
- Crochet Hook
- Yarn Needle
- Fiberfill
- Safety eyes